*Have an AWESOME Day ON PURPOSE...*

*Brina Maria*

All rights reserved. This book is protected under the copyright laws of the United States of America. This book may not be copied or reprinted for commercial gain or profit. The use of short quotations or occasional page copying for personal or group study is permitted and encouraged. Permission will be granted upon request. Unless otherwise identified.

Book Cover Design by:

DESTINED PUBLISHING

DestinedPublishing@outlook.com

© *Copyright 2017. All rights reserved.*

*By Brina Maria*

ISBN-13: 978-1548192099
ISBN-10: 1548192090

## *Dedication*

*To the woman who would often say in song to me, "For the nine months I carried you..." The ONE that believed her only girl would be great in whatever endeavors I set out to achieve. My #1 cheerleader whom I loved to make proud, MY MOMMA,*

*Sheila Michelle Archie!!!
March 8, 1960 ~ July 26, 2010*

## *Acknowledgements*

*The heartbeats of my heart...*
*MY Squad*
*Robert III, Brinia, Ryan, Brinae, & Bella*

*You are the reasons I have shifted gears into full speed ahead. You are why I am compelled to NOT give up. You all are the encouragement I need to LIVE, ON PURPOSE!!!*

## *Introduction*

*As a working, single woman, and mother of five, I get lazy, tired, and even discouraged at times. What pushes me, is that, I have purposed in my mind to not quit, not give up. What I tell myself the most is, "Brina, you CANNOT abort the mission!!!"*

*There is so much PURPOSE in me, I HAVE to get out...*

*As I am writing to you, I am speaking to myself. This book jumped in my spirit as I was driving from Illinois to Niagara Falls in Canada. I decided to take what I call a, "BrinaCation". I was at a point of being mentally exhausted and needed to get away!*

*Being in a serene, peaceful, quiet place helps to calm my mind. I am always trying to figure out the next step of my life. I have to bring my mind to the moment to cherish and embrace it. The world is fast paced as it is, you don't need to be.*

*Live your life creating memories. Part of my happiness comes when I can make others happy. I purpose to not allow anything to steal my joy because I know that I can be anything I want to be. I just want to spend the rest of my days loving on people, and living!!! I want to encourage you to do the same.*

*Our days are numbered here, don't let your flame ever die out.*

> *"I was looking for someone to inspire me, motivate me, support me, and keep me focused… I was looking for someone who would love me, cherish me, and make me happy. I realize, all along I was looking for myself."*
>
> ~From Deep Within

## *Note to You…*

*As you are reading the tidbits I've shared with you, use your journal to write down something that jumps out at you specifically. So, that, when you're having a not so good day, you will be able to reach for what you need to empower you*
*ON PURPOSE…*

*Things to Remind Yourself Daily*

*\* Fill your mouth with LIFE, not death (Stop negative talk)*
*\* Find something to be grateful for and hold on to that*
*\* Positivity is a choice*
*\* Celebrate your individuality*
*\* Prepare to succeed*
*\*Keep striving*
*\*Keep praying*

*Become better

*Be awesome

*I speak goodness over your life. I declare an abundance of greatness for you. My prayer for you, you will be overflowed with astonishing blessings. I declare, as you change your way of thinking for your betterment, your path will align accordingly.*

*Go after things that are purposed for YOU!!! Let's proclaim our destiny! Don't miss out on your next...*

*For the next 30 days, I pray that as you read and meditate, your fire will be sparked to...*

**Have an AWESOME Day ON PURPOSE!!!**

*Have an AWESOME Day ON PURPOSE...*

## *Day 1*
## *Purpose...*

*YOU were created on purpose for a purpose. You were designed for greatness. It's not by coincidence that you were born. There is something special about you. There's a certain assignment that can only be fulfilled by you.*

*Have you ever wondered, "Why wasn't I born in the years past?" The simple answer is... You weren't needed then. Your birth date is when your purpose manifested into time. There is a certain amount of time for you to accomplish the mission in which you were sent here to do it.*

*Each of us have been designed to help someone else. Some hundreds of people, and some just one person. Be what you need to be, to be an asset.*

*You never know how your life can be a joy or hindrance to someone. Oftentimes, the decisions we make for ourselves, can affect another person, so think before the act.*

*Become an asset, not a liability. Remember, there is someone waiting on what's inside of you. That very thing will help them get to where they need to be in this life.*

*There is passion burning inside you to do, stop procrastinating. The world needs to see your purpose.*

*You can change your world by changing you. Go after what you were created for...*

## *Day 1*
## *Affirmation/Declaration*

> *TODAY...*
> *WILL be one of the best days of my life!!!*
> *I choose to continue to walk in my predestined purpose.*
> *I will not allow anything to hinder my process.*
> *I will only focus on things concerning me.*
> *I will make myself a priority.*

**Have an AWESOME Day**
**ON PURPOSE...**

## *Day 2*
## *One Day at a Time…*

*If you're anything like me, you would build Rome in one day!!! Well, the thing about that, you can't!*

*My brain doesn't allow me to think small, and it's constantly on the go. I am always trying to find solutions to problems, trying to figure out how I can accomplish 50,000 things in 16 hours. When I think too much, I accomplish little. "One day at a time", is what I have to tell myself.*

*If you find yourself in anyway like this, you have to learn to prioritize by importance.*

*The greatest thing to consider, YOU matter most.*

*What the world throws at you will/can stress you, don't let it.*

*You need you!!! You are your most significant asset. Everyday take time for you. Learn to breathe, inhale AND exhale. We tend to take it all in, but never release.*

*Releasing is the key to de-stress your life. Just do your part, and the rest will fall in place. Know your limitations. Stop taking on more than you can handle.*

*Stop living in time and live in the moment. Create everlasting memories. "Don't ruin a good today by thinking about a bad yesterday. Let it go."*

## *Day 2*
## *Affirmation/Declaration*

> *TODAY…*
> *WILL be one of the best days of my life!!!*
> *I will focus on what matters most.*
> *If it's out of my control, I won't concern myself with it.*
> *I choose to let go of ALL things that cause me stress.*

***Have an AWESOME Day***
***ON PURPOSE…***

## *Day 3*
## *Enjoy Life…*

*I choose LIFE, therefore, I LIVE…*

*When you were born into this realm, you were born into time. Meaning, there is an expiration on your time here. At a funeral, the one that was giving the eulogy subject was, "What Will You Do with Your Dash?" The dash he spoke of was the time in between your birth and expiration.*

*That started to fill my thoughts with so much I could do, want to do, and needed to do. After pondering over it for about a week, I came up with, "ENJOY LIFE!"*

*Enjoy every waking moment you have here on this earth. Enjoy all of the family and friends you are blessed to have in your life, even the ones that gets on your reserved nerve.*

*Enjoy the path you are on. Remember, you were designed for your path. No, your path will not look like someone else's, you have to make the best of it in order to enjoy it. The journey you're on was uniquely designed just for you.*

*We get caught up in "things", which are temporary fixes, and that's not enjoying life*

*Fill your mouth with life, not death. Don't take what's not going right, and magnify it. Appreciate what IS going right.*

*"Life isn't about finding yourself. Life is about creating yourself." Remember, it's never too late to live happily ever after...*

# *Day 3*
## *Affirmation/Declaration*

> *TODAY...*
>
> *WILL be one of the best days of my life!!!*
> *I will choose to enjoy this life to the fullest by simply living.*
>
> *I choose to keep a positive mindset on what is AWESOME in my life.*
>
> *I choose to live up to my fullest potential.*
>
> *Things are always working out for me.*
>
> *I have the freedom and power to create the life I desire.*

**Have an AWESOME Day**
***ON PURPOSE...***

## Day 4
## *Wake Up & Be Awesome...*

*Sometimes, depending on how you've slept, what you've dreamt about, or even if you already have your mind set on the many tasks you have to complete in that day, can alter how you view the day even before it happens.*

*At the open of your eyes, create how your day is going to turn out by keeping an open mind that today, this day, will be one of the best days of my life.*

*Your best day will differ from the next person's best day. You have the choice to choose the path you want to be on. So, why not choose an awesome one?*

*For example, rain makes me want to either sleep, or cuddle in front of a good movie with hot chocolate and s'mores. Just because it gets me in the mood to do one of the two, I may choose to go out and play in the rain. (I love being in the rain by the way.) But, I have options.*

*You too have a decision to make when you open your eyes. Make TODAY better than yesterday, ON PURPOSE...*

*Don't just survive this life, live this life. Live it to the fullest. Whatever you have to do today, make it AWESOME, make it WONDERFUL!!! Do it with a glad heart, not grudgingly. Pick the emotion that'll have you feeling good, even if the task or situation is something you don't want to do, but have to do.*

## *Day 4*
## *Affirmation/Declaration*

> *TODAY…*
> 
> *WILL be one of the best days of my life!!!*
> *Dear Self, today you will shine.*
> *I am healthy and filled with energy.*
> *I greet this day with confidence and ease.*
> *This day, I will choose to see the bright side in all situations.*
> *Make today so awesome, yesterday gets jealous.*

**Have an AWESOME Day**
**ON PURPOSE…**

## *Day 5*
## *Create Your Happiness...*

*People, places, and things.... Are only to enhance our happiness. Your happiness should come from within and burst outward.*

*When we start to shift the focus on outside sources (not within), we place expectations on them. So, when those things fail us, it oftentimes, "hurt our feelings". Then we want to place the blame, when in actuality, you have no one to blame but yourself. You are responsible for yourself.*

*Yes, when bad things happen, emotions get revved up. But you have the option to opt out of feeling bad.*

*I used to have a major issue, when who I*

*thought should make me happy, didn't. Then, one day, they were gone. I had to come to the conclusion, "If I was depending on them to "make" me happy, now they're gone, will I not be happy anymore?"*

*I went on the search for making myself happy. In doing that, I had to learn me, and I realized, I make 'me' happy!!!*

*When others come along, they can add to it. But, even if they leave, I'm still happy.*

*I found my happy places, and I go there whenever needed. My happy places aren't all physical either. The door to happiness opens from inside. "Happiness is an inside job. Don't assign that much power over your life." I strive to stay in my mental happy places. No, I'm not crazy, JUST HAPPY!!!*

## *Day 5*
## *Affirmation/Declaration*

> *TODAY...*
>
> *WILL be one of the best days of my life!!!*
> *I will choose to search for my inner happiness.*
>
> *I can accomplish whatsoever I put my mind to because I believe in myself.*
>
> *I choose to be happy, no matter what takes place around me.*
>
> *When I find my inner happy place, I will pull from there every time I need to.*

**Have an AWESOME Day**
***ON PURPOSE...***

## *Day 6*
## *Dream Big…*

*I want to build a multi-billion dollar enterprise. I want to become a professional traveler around the world and explore all this earth has to offer. I want to live freely every day of this life. I want to get massages 365 days a year. I want to 'brainwash' people into thinking they are great and can achieve anything they put their mind and work in to!!!*

*Those are some of my many dreams. Because I have this crazy idea that my purpose is bigger and greater than me, I choose to work every waking moment being productive to achieve every goal that I've set for me and my family.*

*I have been blessed to birth five children, and I push myself for them. Part of my purpose is to lead by example when it comes to them. They shall rise up and call me, "blessed."*

*A song I learned as a little girl, "I might as well think big. Why should any thought be small? I might as well think big, if I'm gonna think at all."*

*We have been conditioned to live to work hard. I say, "Work hard to live". You don't have to wait until you retire at an old age, you can retire now! (That's another discussion, budgeting)*

*Thinking is one thing. Believing you can achieve it is something else.*

*Just because of who you are, is ample*

*reason enough to know that you can, and will. Get ready to do the necessary work to get to the places you've dreamt about!!!*

## *Day 6*
## *Affirmation/Declaration*

> *TODAY...*
> *WILL be one of the best days of my life!!!*
> *I believe in myself and my abilities.*
> *I am full of goodness.*
> *I am making space for more success to come in my life.*
> *I am worthy enough to follow my dreams and manifest my desires.*

**Have an AWESOME Day**
**ON PURPOSE...**

## *Day 7*
## *Free Yourself…*

*Have you ever felt like you were trapped? Sometimes you feel like your good just isn't good enough, so you stop trying. Stop allowing people to drain you.*

*Well, you hold the keys to your freedom. If anything in your life is keeping you in bondage, unlock the door and walk out!*

*Don't settle for other people's buffoonery. Let them be them without you having to compromise yourself. You don't have a depreciation value stamp on you. Your appreciation level should rise.*

*Ways I've found helpful of freeing yourself…*
*\*Evaluate your self-worth*

*Break the barriers you've created for yourself that keep you imprisoned*

*Be an original*

*Forgive yourself and others*

*Learn to say no*

*Control your reaction to things*

*Love yourself*

*Detach from outcome and focus on the process*

*Let go of toxic relationships*

*Laugh at yourself, laugh at life, and learn not to take it all too seriously.*

*Live, ON PURPOSE!!!*

## *Day 7*
## *Affirmation/Declaration*

> *TODAY...*
>
> *WILL be one of the best days of my life!!!*
> *I will start to become the change that I want to see.*
> *I will walk in favor.*
> *I choose to not entertain buffoonery.*
> *I will let go of anything that will hinder my self-growth.*
> *I release all grudges, bitterness, and hurt.*
> *I am free from my past.*

**Have an AWESOME Day**
**ON PURPOSE...**

## *Day 8*
## *Train Your Mind to See the Good...*

*Think about how you think about things...*

*Even bad has its purpose in your destiny. WHAT?! Did I just read what I thought I just read? YES!!! Again, even bad has its purpose in your course of life. Without it, you won't appreciate the good in your life. Don't let a breakdown break you down.*

*I commonly say, "What I go through is not just for me, but for someone else." I strive to help in any way possible. If my experiences can be of assistance to you, by all means, let it.*

*When life happens to us, it's all for a lesson. It's up to you to learn the lesson and live accordingly. Until you learn whatever lesson you need to learn to move forward on your path, you'll keep repeating it.*

*Start looking at life as a lesson. Today will help prepare you for tomorrow. Each circumstance is a step to your growth. Each step is development for your purpose.*

*Choose, on purpose, to overlook the bad, and seek for the good...*

## *Day 8*
## *Affirmation/Declaration*

> *TODAY...*
> *WILL be one of the best days of my life!!!*
> *I let go of all negativity that rests in my body and mind.*
> *I believe in the good things coming.*
> *I will take each phase of my life as a stepping mount for my journey.*
> *I will not allow anything to stifle my growth process.*
> *I choose to progress.*

**Have an AWESOME Day**
***ON PURPOSE...***

## Day 9
### Choose Peace...

*In a world of chaos, sometimes you want to run and hide, seclude yourself from EVERYTHING... How can one find or even have peace with so many obstacles, so many disturbances, and so many traumatic happenings going on? Peace comes from within. YOU have to calm yourself from the inside. The moment you weed out the noise, invite tranquility in.*

*Find a calm place, and rest there. One of my physical places that I go to is anywhere there's a body of water (lake, beach, even the aquarium, etc.). I'll sit and watch the water overlap itself, the birds as they fly low to fish for food, the sun gazing it's brightness onto the water. If I could live on water, I probably would. Times that I can't get to the water, I visualize it in my head, taking me there mentally.*

*Places of tranquility tends to take your mind off of being bogged down. Take a walk in the park, walk on any natural surface with bare feet to connect with nature. Studies show that walking barefoot has many benefits, including decreasing of emotional anxiety.*

*Listen to music with no lyrics (jazz, spa, instrumentals). Listening to music would be my remedy for everything. Pray. Meditate. Spend time alone. When it rains, sit and listen to the rain drops.*

*There will be times when faced with frustration, the initial thought might be react. It's all about finding the calm in the chaos. Choosing peace ON PURPOSE, is already having a mindset, that whatever comes, peace will get the best of me.*

*"Inner peace begins the moment you choose not to allow another person or event to control your emotions..."*

## *Day 9*
## *Affirmation/Declaration*

> *TODAY...*
> *WILL be one of the best days of my life!!!*
> *I choose to have peace wherever I am.*
> *I won't worry about the things I can't control.*
> *I will purposely remove myself from chaotic situations.*
> *I will relax my mind and spirit.*

***Have an AWESOME Day ON PURPOSE...***

## *Day 10*
## *Feed Your Focus...*

*Funny thing about this day... As I was sitting in front of my laptop to write this day, I got stuck on social media. When I looked up, 23 minutes had passed and all I had written were the first two paragraphs.*

*It's very easy to lose sight of the plan/mission. "If you aim at nothing, you will hit it every time." You must have something in front of you in order to reach for it. Otherwise, you'll be in 'zombie' mode.*

*The first thing to ask, "What is your focus?" Once you have prioritized what's more important to you, set your eyes on that.*

*Don't allow yourself to become easily*

*distracted. Remember you are striving to get somewhere. Don't stop until you get there. Even after that, go to the next place.*

*Spend time everyday working to accomplish what you have set out to do. Sacrifice play time. My suggestion would be to set a certain amount of time, even a set time each day, to work on what you're trying to complete.*

*Remember, you have purpose, that's the reason you were born…*

*"One day you'll look back and realize that you worried too much about things that didn't really matter." Stop looking back, unless you're pulling from the lessons you've learned. Growth is your goal, don't become stagnant.*

## *Day 10*
## *Affirmation/Declaration*

> *TODAY...*
> *WILL be one of the best days of my life!!!*
> *Things are always working out for me.*
> *I choose to focus on peace.*
> *I will remain balanced in what's really important to me.*
> *I choose to align my thoughts on what will get me to my next levels.*

**Have an AWESOME Day**
**ON PURPOSE...**

## *Day 11*
## *Be Fearlessly Authentic…*

*I've heard people say, "You are a designer's original". Well, yes you are. You are uniquely made, no duplications. There is only one of you, even if you were a twin, you are still YOU.*

*There are qualities in you, others can't possess. You are a rare jewel. Although your distinctiveness may not all the time be appreciated or even noticed, YOU notice it!!!*

*Not one single person on this earth can duplicate you, imitate, but it's still not the original.*

*You are indistinguishable, valuable, and*

*needed. You may be compared, but you're not comparable. You are an asset, not a liability. What you carry inside is sure to spark the fire in someone else.*

*Your authenticity is pure. You are wonderfully sculptured, inside and out. There is nothing inaccurate about you.*

*Live with confidence. Let go of pride and ego. Walk in your natural born right of being one of a kind.*

*How you see you is how you are seen...*

## *Day 11*
## *Affirmation/Declaration*

> *TODAY...*
> *WILL be one of the best days of my life!!!*
> *I am overflowing with positivity.*
> *I possess the ability to lead and inspire.*
> *I shall no longer allow negative thoughts or feelings to drain me of my energy.*
> *I shall walk in my greatness.*

**Have an AWESOME Day**
**ON PURPOSE...**

## *Day 12*
## *Love on Someone…*

*Outside of loving yourself, love on someone.*

*Think love… Speak love… Feel love… Share love… Spread love… Do Love… Be love…*

*"People grow when they are loved well. If you want to help others heal, love them without an agenda."*

*There is a tremendous lack of love being displayed in today's world. It seems, because people don't know how to love. There are a ton of hurting people, that's hurting so, they wouldn't know love if it slapped them in the face.*

*Well, you can be the love that can pull them*

*out. Love on them as if they've never been hurt. "You ARE love. You come from love, and your natural state is to BE love." Love empowers to higher levels.*

*"Dare to unconditionally love every person, including yourself. Become the energy of love." Someone said, "Throw love around like confetti wherever you go!!!"*

*Did you know that part of your purpose is to love? Go, be love. Wear love everywhere you go. The world needs you. Let all that you do, be done in love. Don't love to be loved, love to love...*

*Love, ON PURPOSE...*

## *Day 12*
## *Affirmation/Declaration*

---

*TODAY...*

*WILL be one of the best days of my life!!!*
*I will not take for granted the things that matter the most to me.*
*I will not just say love, I will do love and be love.*

---

**Have an AWESOME Day**
**ON PURPOSE...**

## *Day 13*
## *Be You & Do You...*

*This is one of my favorite mottos. Be you and do you is simply just that.*

*We live a society where nearly everything comes with structured rules, dictating what you can and cannot do, what you can say and not say, what you can wear without being degraded or shamed, even down to the type of job you can have, and so on...*

*"When you are born, your name is decided for you, your nationality, your religion, and sect are also given to you. Then you spend the rest of your life defending something you didn't even choose." When I read that, that was a 'wow' moment.*

*It was not until I was 35, I realized how much of my life I'd spent conforming, which didn't always feel right.*

*Another quote I read, "When you are born in a world you don't fit in; it's because you were born to help create a new one." Now that jumped out at me! So, for the next few years after that, I was on a search for my individuality, and will encourage anyone to do the same.*

*By the age of 37, I felt at my freest!!! I was on a path of deprogramming my mind just to live on purpose, without all of the man-made restrictions I'd been accustomed to.*

*Set your own limitations. I know I'll get a few eyes rolled because of that statement.*

*But guess what, you can do everything right and still, people will have something negative to say.*

*When you start to venture off your path, trust me, you'll know it. Just get back in line...*

*"Life only comes around once, so do whatever makes you happy, and be with whoever makes you smile."*

*Take the limits off...*

## *Day 13*
## *Affirmation/Declaration*

> *TODAY...*
> *WILL be one of the best days of my life!!!*
> *I have the power to create change.*
> *I choose to change the negative way I view life itself.*
> *I will respond with a positive mindset.*
> *All is well in my world.*

**Have an AWESOME Day**
**ON PURPOSE...**

## *Day 14*
## *Commit to Yourself...*

*"I am not saying 'no' to you. I am simply saying 'yes' to me."*

*How much less should you love yourself? Don't look for anyone to validate how you should be loved. Instead of conforming to what feels comfortable, be in control of how you are loved.*

*If you continue to sacrifice what you want/desire, you'll regret it later. Love yourself enough to walk from anything that's unhealthy.*

*You are AWESOME!!! You can have whatever you desire, because that's the atmosphere you will create for yourself.*

*Don't renege on yourself. Don't give up on you. See where you want to be, and go there. Do the work it takes to get to the next levels.*

*Choosing you as priority is not being selfish at all. Learn to only say 'yes' to the people and situations that are good for your emotional and physical well-being.*

*Before you commit to anyone or anything, you need to commit to yourself...*

*"The more you love yourself, the less nonsense you'll tolerate."*

## *Day 14*
## *Affirmation/Declaration*

> *TODAY...*
> *WILL be one of the best days of my life!!!*
> *I will work on my personal goals.*
> *I choose to work on becoming a better me.*
> *I will live the way it's intended for me to live, in the overflow.*
> *I will plan the work and begin to work the plan that will get me to my next level.*
> *Today, I choose me.*

### *Have an AWESOME Day ON PURPOSE...*

## *Day 15*
## *Just Breathe...*

*Inhale... Exhale... Breathe in... Breathe out... Relax... Calm down... Compose oneself... Let oneself go... Loosen up... Put one's feet up... Repose... Rest... Sit back... Sit down... Take a break... Take your time... Time out... Unwind... Take a load off... Lighten up...*

*These are things that have become rare these days. We live in a fast paced world. Always on the go, always something to do, always something to get done.*

*I made a to-do list every night before I went to bed, focusing on what I needed to do the next day. Then, spent the entire day fulfilling the list. After the list was done, it was time to do the things that weren't on the list.*

*After running myself almost to the ground, I had to realize: 1. I'm one person, 2. Nothing will get done if I stress myself to the point of being sick, 3. Everything is not priority.*

*When I started a membership at the local massage parlor, I had to get a minimum of two hours each session. It literally took a little over an hour just for me to relax, being uptight for so long.*

*Once I learned to 'breathe' more often, I can go in and get an hour and it feels like I've been there for hours.*

*Getting things done, and relaxing goes hand-in-hand. Finding balance is key.*

*Working to attain a goal, but never taking time for your body to wind down, will cause more damage. Breathe!!!!*

## *Day 15*
## *Affirmation/Declaration*

> *TODAY...*
> *WILL be one of the best days of my life!!!*
> *I lovingly release myself from my own past...*
> *I choose to live in the authority that has been given to me.*
> *I will take time to relax.*
> *I will give myself room to breathe.*

***Have an AWESOME Day***
***ON PURPOSE...***

## *Day 16*
## *Create Your Own Sunshine…*

*"Maybe the journey isn't so much about becoming anything. Maybe it's about unbecoming everything that isn't really you, so you can be who you were meant to be in the first place."*

*This spoke high volume to me. After being conditioned to your family's traditions and morals, you think that's the end of your learning. Truth of the matter, it was just the beginning of a stepping stone.*

*Another quote, "The deeper you go within yourself, the more you begin to realize that you are far more powerful than you have been permitted to believe." This was a 'wow' moment for me!!!*

*Until a few years ago, I walked the path that my family created for me. I dealt with two major losses in my life, the death of my mother and the experience of divorce.*

*I spent my years being in a shadow. It wasn't until those two life changing obstacles, that I came to the conclusion of living in my own sunshine.*

*No longer were either of them here to help lead and guide me. This was the beginning of an entirely new journey.*

*"I want to inspire people… I want someone to look at me and say, 'Because of you, I didn't give up.'" You too can be the breath of fresh air to someone. Let your sun shine bright enough that a lost person will find their way.*

## *Day 16*
## *Affirmation/Declaration*

> *TODAY...*
> *WILL be one of the best days of my life!!!*
> *The sun I build for myself will shine even in dark places.*
> *I will be the light for others.*
> *I will wear a smile so bright, it will cause even the saddest person to smile.*
> *I will be stress-free.*
> *I make me happy!!!*

**Have an AWESOME Day**
***ON PURPOSE...***

## *Day 17*
## *Today is a Perfect Day for a New Beginning…*

*"You know all the things you've always wanted to do? You should go do them."*

*One thing about life, you have a free will to make whatever decisions you choose. All of which aren't good ones. But, the experiences are for learning.*

*Let go of the past and embrace what's to come. Your mind has to arrive at your destination before your life does. You have to see yourself there before you get there.*

*Having a vision is key. With it, brings you to have something to look forward to, reach for, and work on.*

*Remember, just because your past didn't turn out the way you might've wanted it to, doesn't mean your future can't be better than you've ever imagined.*

*I read a quote, "Speak what you seek until you see what you've said." That was a "WOW" moment for me. Another one I've heard, "Say what you heard, so you can see what you said."*

*The thought/idea comes to mind, replay it by saying it, then the atmosphere will be set for it to start manifesting!!!*

*"The way to get started is to quit talking and begin doing." Where you are today should not be where you are tomorrow. Step into the growth process every day.*

*"Your future is not ahead of you, it's trapped within you. Release your future and manifest your destiny."*

*"If you don't take the time to design and plan your life, you will have to settle for what life gives you..."* Joe Duncan

# Day 17
## Affirmation/Declaration

> *TODAY...*
>
> *WILL be one of the best days of my life!!!*
>
> *I love and approve myself...*
>
> *I will get in position for greater.*
>
> *I will not overthink or over work myself by getting the necessary rest for my body.*
>
> *I will think a new thought.*

**Have an AWESOME Day**
***ON PURPOSE...***

## *Day 18*
## ***Believe In the Person You Want To Become…***

*If you go there in the mind, you go there in the body…*

*Never allow anyone to devalue you, by treating you like you're not valuable. Know who you are. Set your standards and follow them! If they can't handle you properly, they're not fit for you…*

*"Stop being afraid of what could go wrong and start being positive of what could go right." This was what held me back for a long time. I didn't believe in me. I knew I was blessed with so many skills and talents. I would work them, but not to my full capacity.*

*My goal is to entrepreneur five businesses, one for each of my children. I have launched three of five, worked, and then stopped for a period of time. Life happened... I had to regain my zeal again.*

*Once I regained the enthusiasm, I allowed nothing to stop me. Yes, curve balls started being thrown, my determination was greater. This book is the first of many missions that will be achieved.*

*I actually look in the mirror and talk to the one I see. You are your greatest cheerleader. Encourage yourself. By the way, you are the one that have the qualities to do what needs to be done. Allow today to prepare you for tomorrow. No more procrastinating or giving up. Plan to outdo your past, not other people.*

## *Day 18*
## *Affirmation/Declaration*

> *TODAY...*
> *WILL be one of the best days of my life!!!*
> *I am accomplished, compassionate, amicable, a finisher, an organizer, manager, producer.*
> *Everything I set my mind to do, I will choose to master it.*
> *I choose to make every dream a reality.*
> *I am ME!!!*

**Have an AWESOME Day**
**ON PURPOSE...**

## Day 19
### *Excuses Doesn't Get Results...*

*I'm too tired. I'm too lazy. I like to procrastinate. I don't have what it takes. It's too difficult. I'm too old. I'm too young. What will people think of me? I'm afraid. No one will notice.*

*What's stopping you up from doing what you really want to do? What's holding you up from being where you really want to be? What's the 'real' reason you haven't completed what you've started?*

*Customarily, we get complacent or too comfortable with being where we are. There is a huge difference in being content where you are and staying where you are because of convenience.*

*"Excuses are monuments of nothingness. They build bridges to nowhere. Those who use these tools of incompetence seldom become anything but nothing at all."* Author Unknown

*In other words, stop with the excuses!!! Either you produce results or excuses, not both.*

*Life is about taking risks. How do you know if you can or can't if you never put in any effort?*

*Step out of your comfort zone. Your fantasies will never become actuality if you don't take the chance of carrying out the plan.*

*Don't let your dreams, visions, or goals die out. Someone is waiting on what's in you...*

## *Day 19*
## *Affirmation/Declaration*

> *TODAY...*
>
> *WILL be one of the best days of my life!!!*
> *I choose to get off my "do-nothing" and do something.*
> *I choose productivity over procrastination.*
> *I choose stability over survival.*
> *I choose winning over settling.*

***Have an AWESOME Day***
***ON PURPOSE...***

## Day 20
## Stay Positive…

*Rise and shine with positive thinking on your mind…*

*Holding on to negative emotions will become draining to your inner man and eventually penetrate to the outside. "Look for something positive in each day, even if some days you have to look a little harder."*

*Keeping an open mind and choosing to surround yourself with positivity will be key. "Sometimes when things are falling apart, they may actually be falling into place."*

*"A positive attitude gives you power over your circumstances instead of your circumstances having power over you."* Joyce Meyer

*You have the ability to control your mind and the way you think. Think on things that are true, honorable, reputable, pure/authentic, lovely, compelling, and gracious. Think on the best, not the worst; the beautiful, not the ugly.*

*"Your body hears everything your mind says." Staying positive doesn't mean things will always turn out good. It is knowing that you will be alright no matter how things turn out.*

*"A positive mind finds opportunity in everything, and a negative mind finds fault in everything." As you think, so shall you be...*

*Think positive, be positive.*

## *Day 20*
## *Affirmation/Declaration*

> *TODAY...*
> *WILL be one of the best days of my life!!!*
> *I will not allow the actions or words of others to change my positive attitude.*
> *I choose to speak positive so the outcome will be positive.*

### *Have an AWESOME Day*
### *ON PURPOSE...*

## *Day 21*
## *Choose Joy…*

*By definition, joy, is the emotion of great delight or happiness caused by something exceptionally good or satisfying. Joy is great happiness, the expression or display of glad feeling.*

*"You create more joy in your life when you let go of worrying about what everyone else thinks."*

*Life itself is a joy. Your experience of life is a unique joy. Seek after the joy in your journey through inspiration. Anything that blocks you from experiencing joy, it's time to let it go.*

*It's okay to take a break from your day-to-day routine, and submerge yourself in what causes your inner man to feel joy.*

*Knowing how great of a mother I am to each of my children, bombards me with an abundant amount of joy. I'm not perfect at being a mother, but I am awesome at motherhood...*

*Everything that causes amazing joy in your world, permit it to resonate or echo loudly within, daily. Joy is not something that just happens. You have to choose it.*

*Joy is not in things, it's in us. "Joy is a decision, a really brave one, about how you are going to respond to life." The same way you choose any emotion, be it, sadness, sorrow, doubt, fear, etc. You too can choose joy!*

*Keep choosing joy...*

## *Day 21*
## *Affirmation/Declaration*

> *TODAY...*
>
> *WILL be one of the best days of my life!!!*
> *I will create a peaceful and loving atmosphere.*
> *I will not allow anything to take my focus on the joy I have.*
> *I will chase after things that will help me stay focused on why I have joy.*

**Have an AWESOME Day**
***ON PURPOSE....***

## *Day 22*
### *Never Stray Away From Yourself...*

*Fall in love with taking care of yourself. No one will protect you more than you will. So stop purposely standing in the line of fire to get hurt.*

*There was a point in my life, I looked to be pained because I had been hurt in multiple ways numerous of times. If good came, I waited on the negative to follow.*

*When you've been scarred so much, you become immune to it, you look for it, even though you hate how it feels.*

*You do not deserve to be bound by what have wronged you. You are not your problems or situations.*

*Straying away from yourself is reneging on your very being. Get to a place where you are comfortable with the awesomeness of yourself.*

*Promise yourself that no matter what life throws your way, you will abstain from giving up. Character is being built and developed when you are going through tough times.*

*Straying away from yourself is straying away from your purpose. It's not a part of your DNA to give up.*

*"When you start seeing your worth, you'll find it harder to stay around people who don't."*

*Be great because you ARE great!!!*

*Be Yourself...*

*Find Yourself...*

*Learn Yourself...*

*Know Yourself...*

*Accept Yourself...*

*Value Yourself...*

*Forgive Yourself...*

*Bless Yourself...*

*Express Yourself...*

*Trust Yourself...*

*Love Yourself...*

*Better Yourself...*

*Believe in Yourself...*

*Empower Yourself...*

## Day 22
## *Affirmation/Declaration*

> *TODAY...*
> *WILL be one of the best days of my life!!!*
> *I choose to love life to the fullest.*
> *I will be content right where I am.*
> *I choose to live by choice, not by chance.*
> *I choose to be useful, not used.*
> *I choose self-esteem, not self-pity.*
> *I choose ME...*

**Have an AWESOME Day**
***ON PURPOSE...***

## *Day 23*
## *Options... Choices... Decisions...*

*Did you know that you don't have to settle? You actually have options. Just because it might "look" or "feel" good, doesn't mean that it's good for you. Choose wisely when following your heart.*

*Oftentimes, we go back and forth in our minds trying to rationalize the pros and cons of a thing, but deep down we already know what should be done. Yes, your heart is saying one thing, but your mind is saying something totally different. Been there, done that.*

*But, again, you already know what to do, especially when you've been down the road before.*

*Don't allow yourself to get stuck. It's ok to ponder for a moment.*

*"But, I want…" It's not about what you want sometimes, it could be what you need. You have to not hold on to things that aren't beneficial to your well-being. Let go, and LIVE!!!*

*Everything you need for your journey will present itself the right way at the most opportune time.*

*Think things through before making decisions. Although time does work against us, be comfortable in your choices.*

## *Day 23*
## *Affirmation/Declaration*

> *TODAY...*
> *WILL be one of the best days of my life!!!*
> *I am in charge of my feelings, and I choose happiness.*
> *Don't be afraid to think a new thought...*
> *Live your life ON PURPOSE with a purpose.*
> *I will learn to make intelligent decisions by weighing all my options.*

**Have an AWESOME Day**
**ON PURPOSE...**

## *Day 24*
## *Choose Happiness…*

*YOU are the key to your OWN happiness. Everything you look for, is inside you already.*

*"If you want to be happy, you have to be happy on purpose. When you wake up, you can't just wait to see what kind of day you'll have. You have to decide what kind of day you'll have."*

*Each day is new opportunity to start over. When you choose happiness over misery, it's satisfying to your spirit. You deserve happiness. You are your only limit. If anything is held back from you, check yourself.*

*You can't allow 'things' to make you happy, there will be times that you may not have 'things'. You can't depend on people to make you happy either. Maybe your expectations exceeds their ability.*

*There's a quote that states, "Happiness is a choice, not a result. Nothing will make you happy until you choose to be happy. No person will make you happy unless you decide to be happy. Your happiness will not come to you. It can only come from you."*
Ralph Marston

## *Day 24*
## *Affirmation/Declaration*

> *TODAY...*
>
> *WILL be one of the best days of my life!!!*
> *I choose to be productive in my personal goals.*
> *I choose to stop all negative flow/energy in my environment.*
> *Even when faced with difficulties, I'll pull from my inner happiness.*

**Have an AWESOME Day**
***ON PURPOSE...***

## *Day 25*
## *Be Love…*

*Purpose in your mind and spirit, today will be a day that I will be love to someone.*

*We've always heard that love is an action word. It's one thing to just verbalize, "I love you", but then put meaning behind and be that love example.*

*There are times when we all need to "feel" loved by someone.*

*Make a conscious effort and decision to make someone's day…*

*\*Pick up the tab of the person behind you in line.*

*Call someone you haven't talked to in a while and tell them, "I just wanted to hear your voice."*

*Pick a fresh flower from the garden (no dirt attached) and give it to a stranger.*

*Write "You Rock" on a napkin and give it to someone to put a smile on their face.*

*When you see someone frowning or in deep thought, SMILE to make them smile.*

* Be a listening ear without judgement.*

*Just randomly start laughing out loud, that will surely get others to start laughing, after they've looked at you with a funny look on their face, trying to figure out why you're laughing hysterically.*

## *Day 25*
## *Affirmation/Declaration*

> *TODAY...*
> *WILL be one of the best days of my life!!!*
> *I will show "love and compassion".*
> *I choose to build up and not tear down.*
> *I will encourage and not discourage.*
> *I will motivate and not dissuade.*

**Have an AWESOME Day**
***ON PURPOSE...***

## *Day 26*
## *You Can…*

*You can BE whatever your mind thinks you can be. You can HAVE whatever your mind thinks you can have. You can GO wherever your mind thinks you can go. You can DO whatever your mind thinks you can do.*

*There's a Proverb that states, "For as he thinketh in his heart, so is he." It all starts with your thinking.*

*In this life, YOU CAN BE AWESOME!!! It all starts in the way you think. If things have not been the way you have desired them to be, it's time to change the way you think. When your thoughts change, your life will change.*

*When you look in the mirror, what do you see? Do you see a person with an "I can" or "I can't" mentality? We tend to give up due to human's validation over us. DON'T!!!*

*First, the seed has to be planted with your thoughts. Then, it can manifest with your actions.*

*People around you can see your greatness, but until you see it, the reality will not come to pass.*

*You possess qualities that weren't put in anyone else. What you have in you, is advantageous.*

*Be what you were created to be. You matter, you ARE important, you ARE needed!!!*

*You are not a failure… You are not a waste of space… You are loved… You are wanted… Believe in yourself… You can do it!!!*

*Let today be the day, no matter the situation around you, know YOU CAN!!!*

# *Day 26*
## *Affirmation/Declaration*

> *TODAY...*
>
> *WILL be one of the best days of my life!!!*
>
> *I choose love over hatred.*
>
> *I choose gratitude over complaining.*
>
> *I choose courage over fear.*
>
> *I choose victory over defeat.*
>
> *I choose forgiveness over bitterness (anger).*
>
> *I will take the limits off!!!*

**Have an AWESOME Day**
**ON PURPOSE...**

## Day 27
## I Am Not For Everyone…

*"You have to get so sure of who you are, that no one's opinion, rejection, or bad behavior, can rock you."*

*Everyone will not have your best interest at heart. Everyone that have come across my path, were definitely for a reason. Some were brief involvements, while others, long term. Whichever, it was predestined.*

*When you embrace each lesson that one brings, the more you'll understand the foreordained path.*

*Whether you helped them, or they you, that purpose was fulfilled. We look at help as always being positive, and to a certain extent.*

*If someone has come into your life and wreaked havoc, take it as a help. How?! Trust there's a lesson in even that. The experience can open your eyes to see multiple things and serve as good in future encounters.*

*Everyone is not meant to hold a close place. Learn people for who they are, and deal accordingly. People will show you themselves. Take heed to any warning signs.*

*Some people that come in your life, is just an assignment for you... Everyone isn't meant for long term. Those that are a part of your present, will not be there in your future. Some will become just a memory. Be wise in your relationships.*

*Love on yourself more. . .*

## *Day 27*
## *Affirmation/Declaration*

> *TODAY...*
> *WILL be one of the best days of my life!!!*
> *I love myself deeply and unconditionally.*
> *I choose kindness over anger.*
> *I choose self-love over self-doubt.*
> *I will be wise in who I allow to entertain me.*

**Have an AWESOME Day**
***ON PURPOSE...***

## *Day 28*
## *Be Productive…*

*Have you ever gotten so frustrated because what you're doing right now is not what you were destined to do, it's not enough? You feel like there's more?*

*It's time to declutter your mind, and focus on your predestined purpose.*

*What you were created for, has purpose for someone else. The longer you procrastinate, the longer they have to wait. It's not about you. Be a blessing to the lives you have to reach.*

*Ask yourself, "How can I be of assistance in being a stepping stone?" Ponder on that a bit.*

*The answer will come to you, if it already hasn't.*

*One of my favorite mottos, "Plan the Work, and Work the Plan" has been instrumental in me moving forward. You always need a strategic plan before getting out there, otherwise, from experience, you will be all over the place.*

*See yourself where you want to be first. Then, get there. Don't waste more time just thinking than doing...*

## *Day 28*
## *Affirmation/Declaration*

> *TODAY...*
>
> *WILL be one of the best days of my life!!!*
>
> *I will have what I decree.*
>
> *I will lead by example.*
>
> *I choose to work more, and efficiently.*
>
> *I will produce results.*

## **Have an AWESOME Day**
## **ON PURPOSE...**

## *Day 29*
## *I Am...*

*Great... Loving... Kind... Smart... Wise...*

*Knowledgeable... Beautiful... Amazing...*

*Intelligent... Blessed... Talented... Gifted...*

*Pulchritudinous... Awe-inspiring...*

*Enjoyable... Humble... Munificent...*

*Successful... Conspicuous... Elegant...*

*Accomplished... Nimble... Compassionate...*

*Amicable... Finisher... Organizer...*

*Manager... Producer... Peace...*

*Appreciative... Dependable... Grateful...*

*Strength... Joy... Happiness... Confident...*

*Loved... Secure... Strong... Faithful...*

*Stable... Immovable... Strong-willed...*

*Bold... Affectionate... Thankful...*

*Fearless... Great... Beneficial... Helpful...*

*Lively... Visionary... Ambitious... Positive...*

*Compassionate... Affectionate...*

*Respectful... Generous... Magnanimous...*

*Marvelous... Adored... Content...*

*Favored... Leader... Inspiring...*

*Entrepreneur... Boss... Determined...*

*Loyal... Attentive... Intelligent... Unique...*

*Original...Healthy... Special... Loveable...*

*Joyous... Fabulous... Wonderful...*

*Courageous... Caring... Giving...*

*Outstanding... Peace... Abundance...*

*Brilliant... Leadership... Integrity...*

***I AM Purposeful!!!***
***I AM ME!!!***

## *Day 29*
## *Affirmation/Declaration*

*TODAY...*

*WILL be one of the best days of my life!!!*

*I will speak life into every dead situation.*

*I choose to walk in my divine favor.*

*I recognize the awesomeness of myself.*

*I will find myself productively busy every day.*

*I will complete my mission.*

*I will be the best original version of ME!*

**Have an AWESOME Day**
**ON PURPOSE...**

## Day 30

*Today will be an AWESOME day!!! How do I know? Because I command it to be, ON PURPOSE...*

*Yes, I have that authority. Death and life are in the power of my tongue. I will be careful of the seeds that I plant with my words.*
*I speak life, therefore, I live!!!*

*I design the atmosphere that I shall reside in. That will be a space of love, joy, peace, happiness. I will look at life as an adventure of lessons and assignments that I will ace.*

*Nothing negative will get the best of me.*

*I was designed for purpose, and that purpose will be fulfilled, in me and through me.*

*I will be the example that someone needs. I recognize that I'm not perfect because I'm human, but yet, I am great because I am human. I don't always get things right, but it's alright. I will take what I've learned today and apply it where needed.*

*What I want does exist.*
*I choose not to settle until I get it.*

*I will not hold on to grudges because I realize that no one gets it right all the time. We are what man deem as flawed, however, I will accept people for who they are, by not placing my personal expectations or judgement on them.*

*If one doesn't have as much knowledge as I have acquired, I dare not down them, but simply share with love.*

*I will cherish and appreciate those sent in my life. I will not take their purpose in my life for granted.*

*I will be grateful for where I am, and excited about where I'm going because my future is in me. I have the keys to unlock every door I need opened.*

*I will love. I will be love.
I will do love. I am love...*

*Have an AWESOME Day
ON PURPOSE...*

*Have an AWESOME Day ON PURPOSE…*

Made in the USA
Lexington, KY
09 September 2017